My Senses

By C.E. Bear
illustrated by Bob Holt

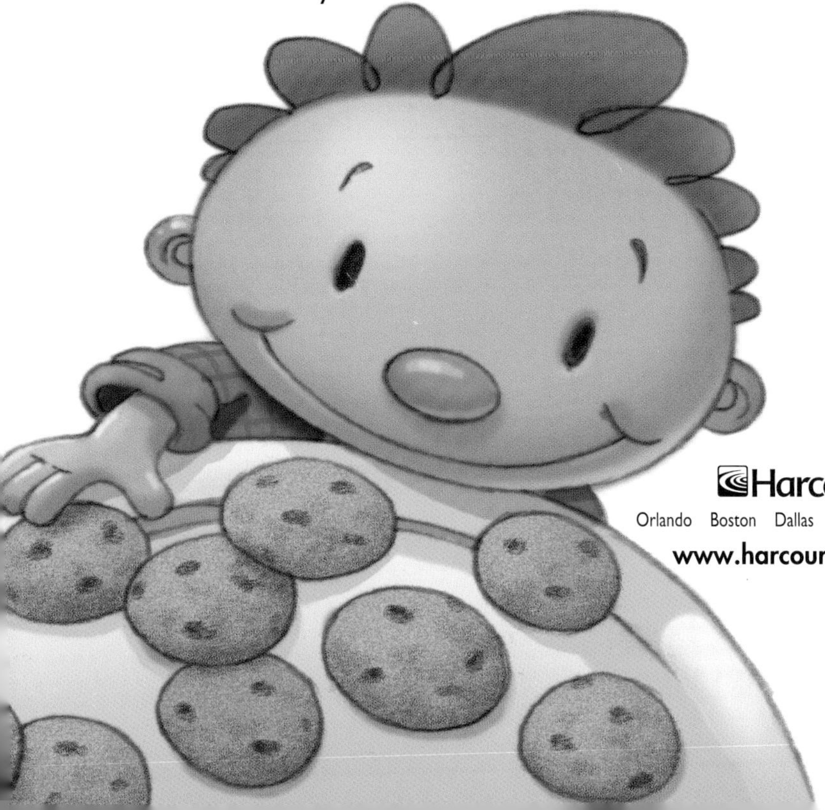

Harcourt
Orlando Boston Dallas Chicago San Diego
www.harcourtschool.com

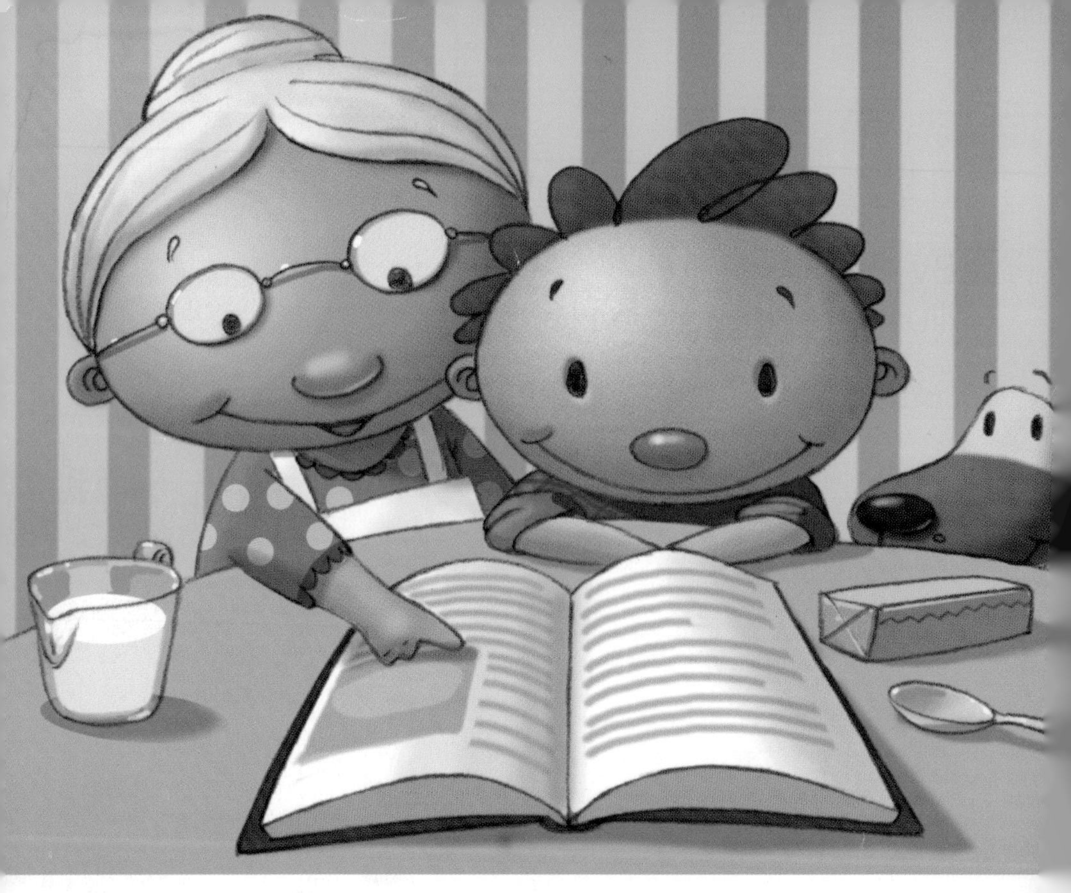

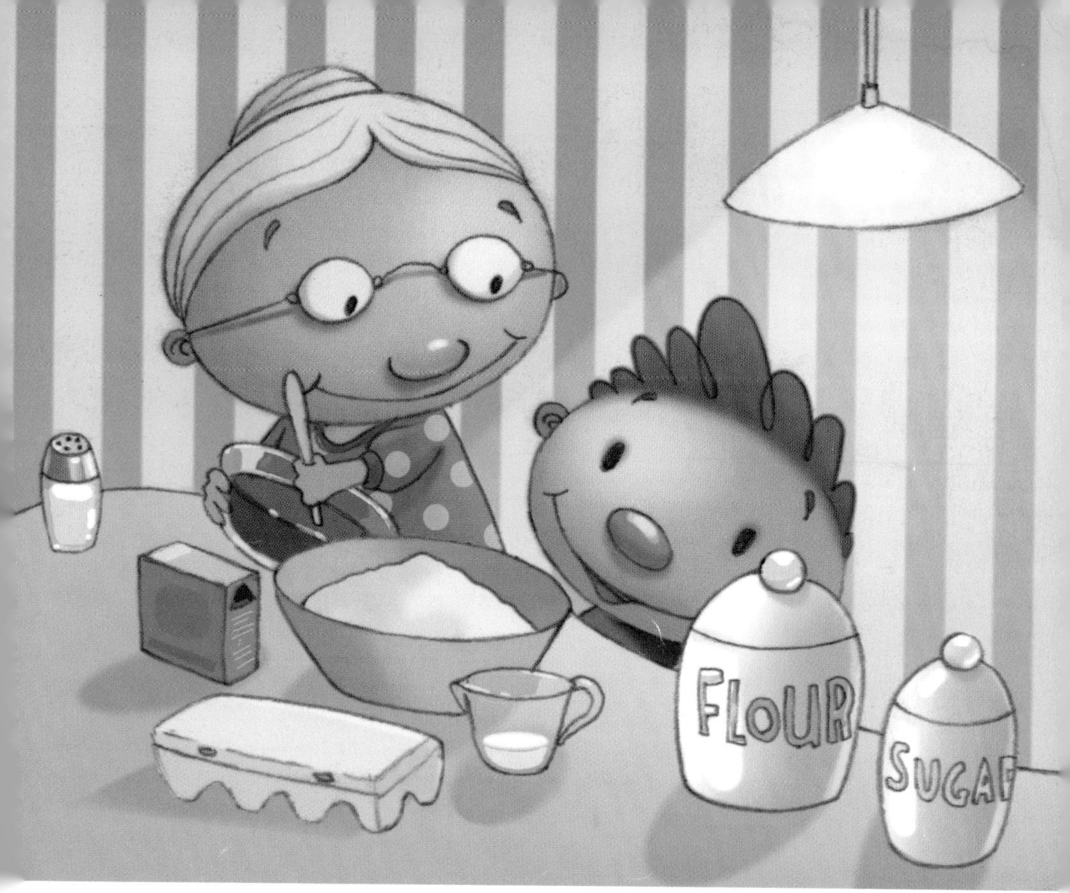

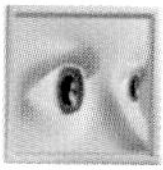

I see.

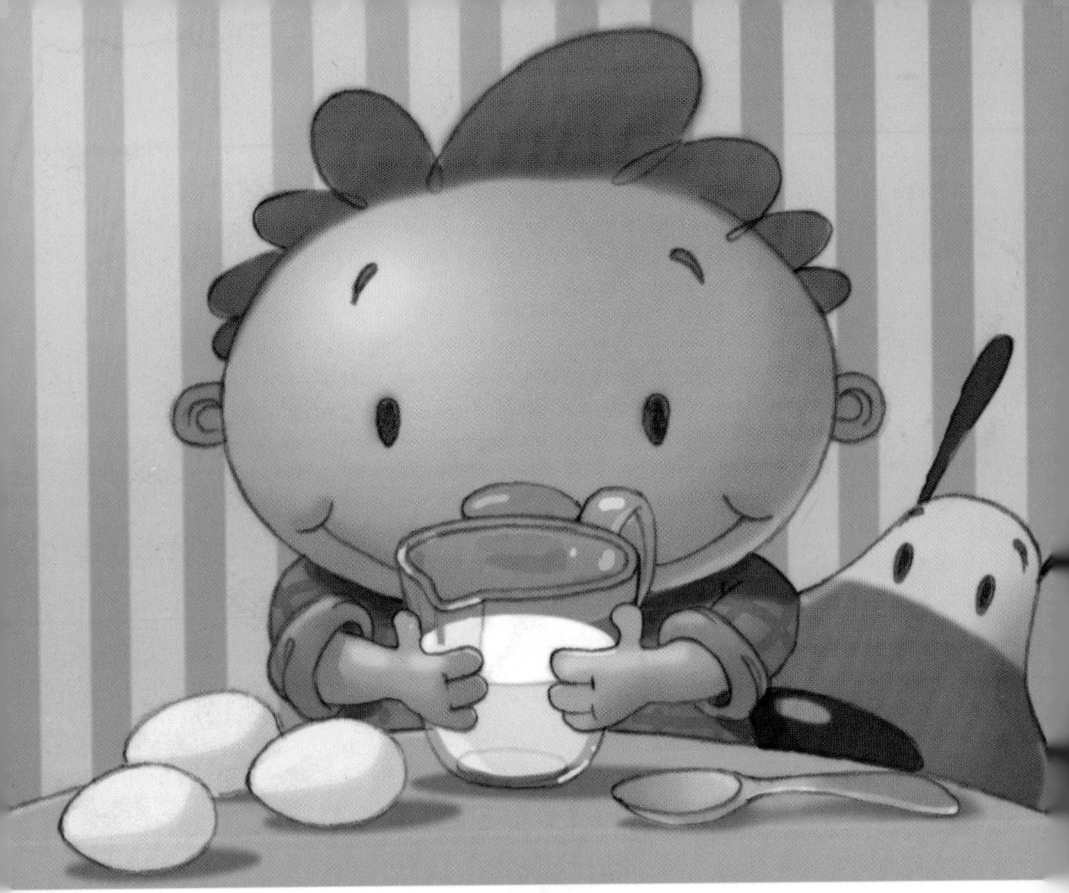

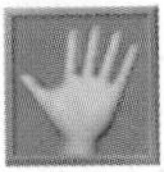

I touch.

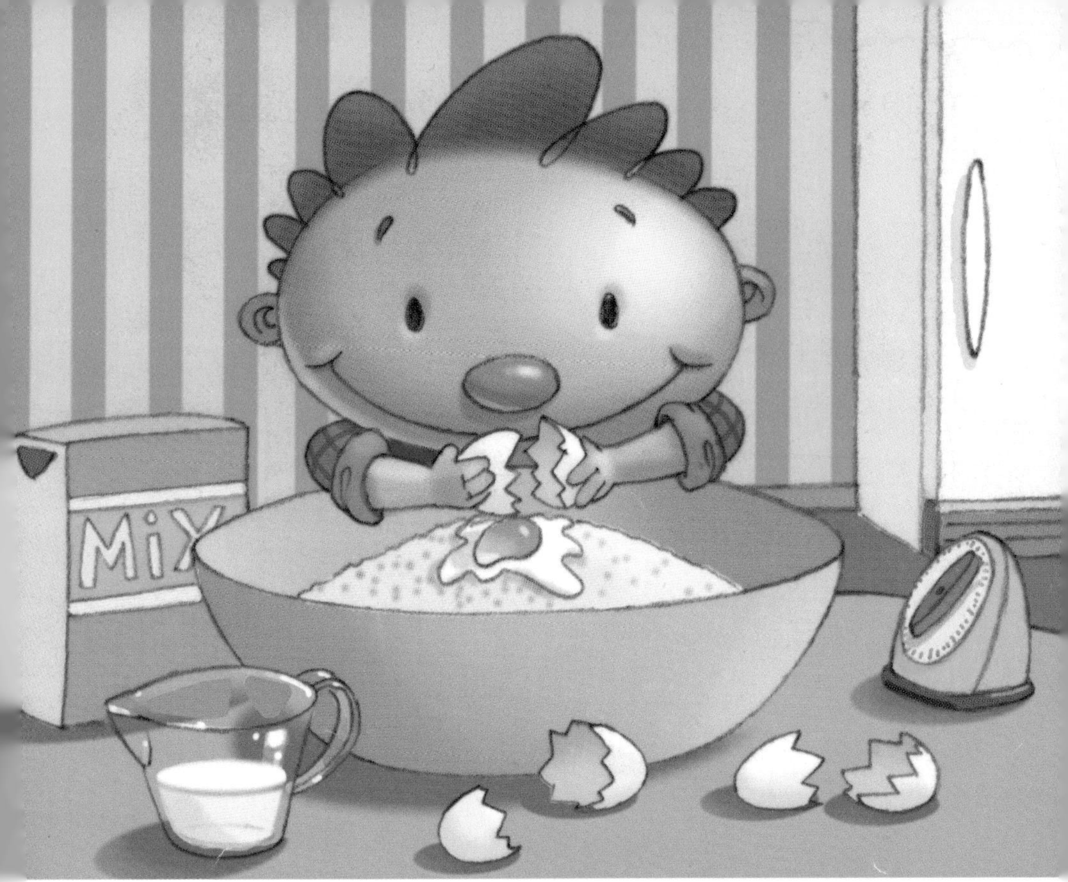

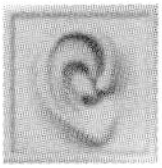

I hear.

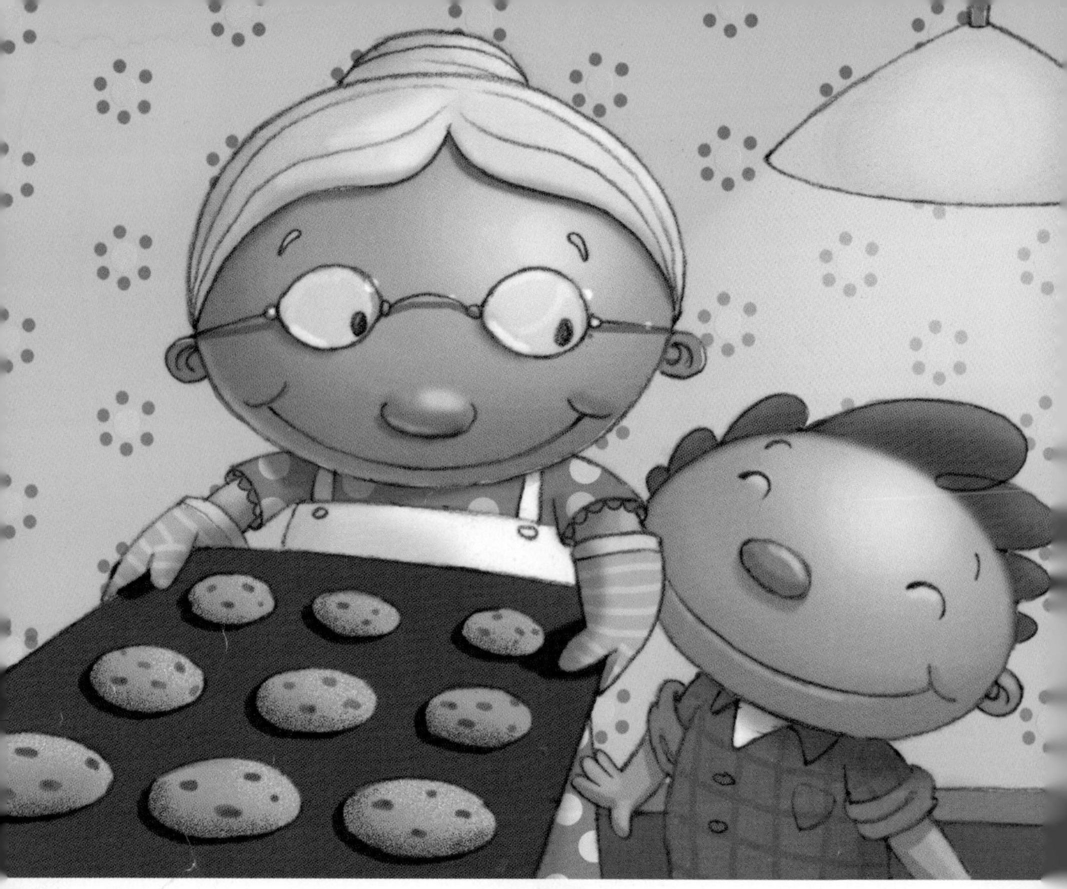

I smell.

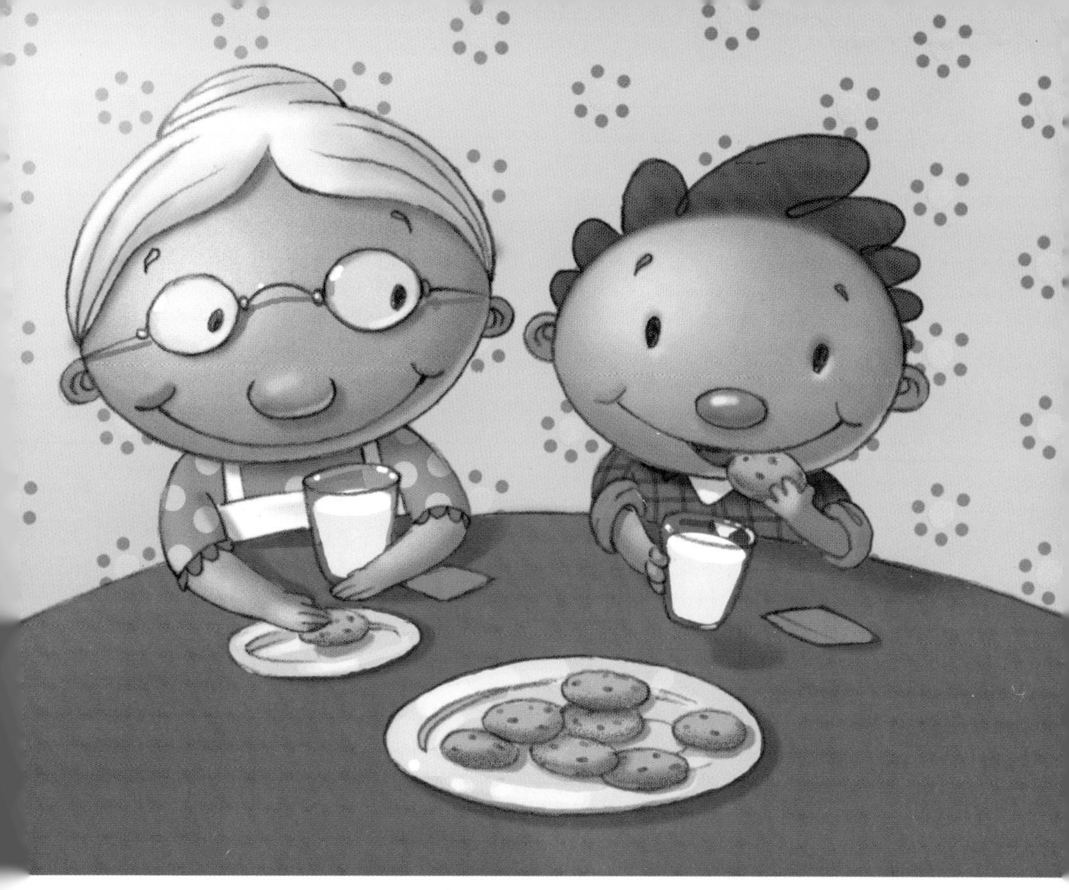

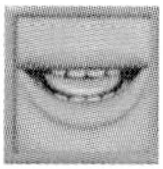

I taste.

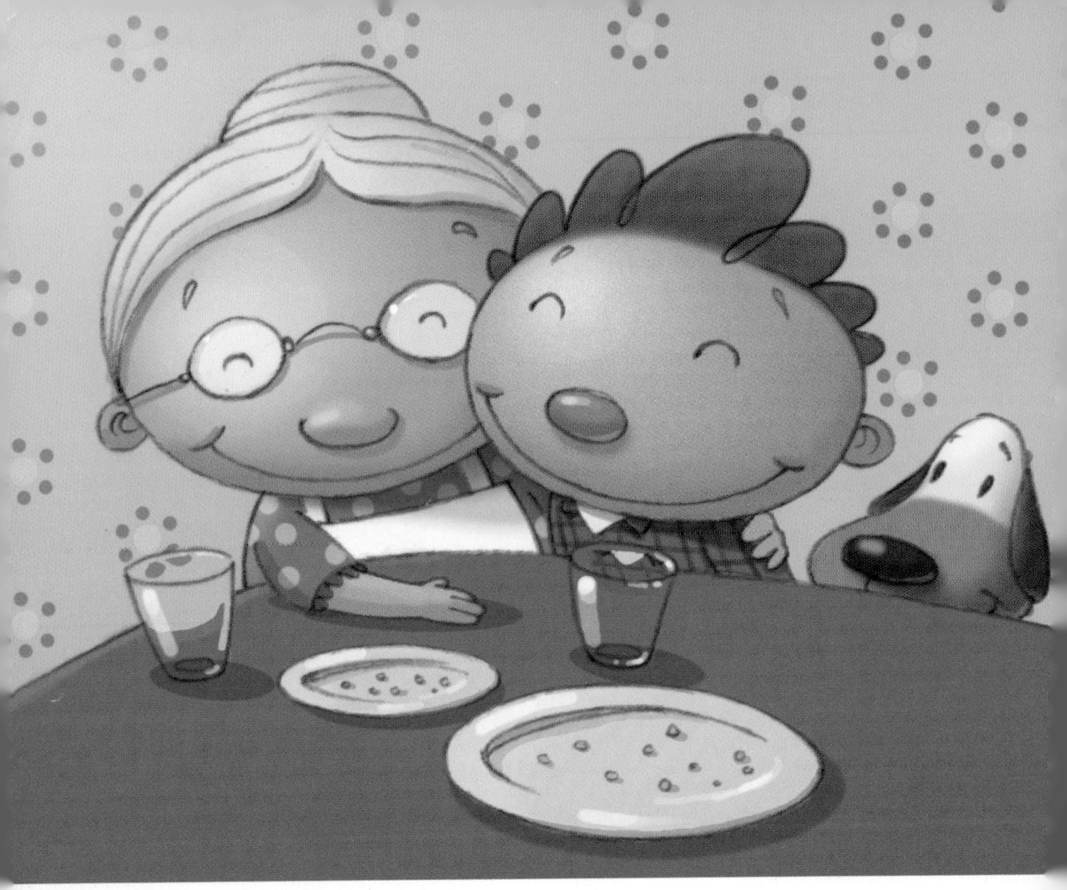